MW01139335

Superstars
of the
OKLAHOMA CITY
THUNDER

by Max Hammer

AMICUS HIGH INTEREST ◆ AMICUS INK

Amicus High Interest and Amicus Ink
are imprints of Amicus
P.O. Box 1329, Mankato, MN 56002
www.amicuspublishing.us

Library of Congress Cataloging-in-Publication Data
Hammer, Max.
  Superstars of the Oklahoma City Thunder / by Max Hammer.
      pages cm. -- (Pro sports superstars (NBA))
  Includes index.
  ISBN 978-1-60753-768-7 (library binding)
  ISBN 978-1-60753-867-7 (ebook)
  ISBN 978-1-68152-022-3 (paperback)
  1. Oklahoma City Thunder (Basketball team)--History--Juvenile literature.
2. Basketball players--United States--Biography--Juvenile literature. I.
Title.
  GV885.52.O37H36 2015
  796.323'640976638--dc23
                              2014045260

Photo Credits: Jim Cowsert/AP Images, cover; Charles Rex Arbogast/AP
Images, 2, 20–21; AP Images, 5, 22; John G. Zimmerman/Sports Illustrated
Classic/Getty Images, 6; Walter Iooss Jr./Sports Illustrated/Getty Images,
9; Rick Stewart/Getty Images, 10; John Froschauer/AP Images, 13;
Christobal Perez/AP Images, 14; Mark J. Terrill/AP Images, 16–17, 19

Produced for Amicus by The Peterson Publishing Company
and Red Line Editorial.

Designer Becky Daum
Printed in Malaysia

HC 10 9 8 7 6 5 4 3 2 1
PB 10 9 8 7 6 5 4 3 2 1

TABLE OF CONTENTS

MEET THE OKLAHOMA CITY THUNDER

The Thunder moved to Oklahoma City in 2008. Before that they played in Seattle. Their name was the SuperSonics. Fans called them the Sonics. The team has had many stars. Here are some of the best.

FRED BROWN

Fred Brown scored many points. He hit shots from far away. Brown helped the Sonics win their first **NBA title**. That was in 1979.

Brown hit more three-point shots than anyone else in 1979.

JACK SIKMA

Jack Sikma was a good shooter. He was also a great defender. He grabbed **rebounds**. Sikma helped Seattle win its 1979 title.

Sikma holds the team record for rebounds.

NATE McMILLAN

Nate McMillan joined the team in 1986. He was a great team player. He often had more **assists** than points.

Fans called McMillan "Mr. Sonic."

GARY PAYTON

Gary Payton was a leader. He played hard. He stopped opponents on **defense**. Payton could score too. He used his strength to get to the hoop.

Payton played for 13 seasons with the Sonics. He left in 2003.

13

SHAWN KEMP

Few could leap like Shawn Kemp. He jumped high for **slam dunks**. He was hard to stop. Kemp helped the Sonics reach the NBA Finals. That was in 1996.

In 1989 Kemp was the youngest player in the NBA. He was 21.

RAY ALLEN

Ray Allen was a natural shooter. Many people copy his style. He could shoot from far away. He led the NBA in three-pointers in 2005-06.

Allen sank more three-pointers than any player.

17

KEVIN DURANT

Kevin Durant joined the team in 2007. He can score from anywhere. He drives to the hoop for **layups**. He sinks **jump shots**. Durant led the NBA in scoring four times.

Durant was the NBA MVP in 2014.

RUSSELL WESTBROOK

Russell Westbrook sets up many plays. His passes help teammates score. But he makes baskets too. He helped the Thunder reach the NBA Finals in 2012.

The Thunder have had many great superstars. Who will be next?

TEAM FAST FACTS

Founded: 1967 as Seattle Supersonics; became Oklahoma City Thunder in 2008

Home Arena: Chesapeake Energy Arena in Oklahoma City, Oklahoma

Mascot: Rumble the Bison

Leading Scorer: Gary Payton (18,207)

NBA Championships: 1 (1979)

Hall of Fame Players: 6, including Gary Payton

WORDS TO KNOW

assist – a pass to a teammate who scores

defense – stopping the other team from scoring

jump shot – a shot taken after jumping in the air

layup – a one-handed shot made after leaping up from beneath the basket

MVP – Most Valuable Player; an honor given to the best player in the NBA each season

NBA – the National Basketball Association

rebound – a ball that bounces away from the basket after a missed shot

slam dunk – a shot in which the player jumps high and throws the ball down through the rim

title – an NBA championship victory

LEARN MORE

Books

Bodden, Valerie. *Kevin Durant (The Big Time)*. Mankato, Minn.: Creative Education, 2014.

Stewart, Mark. *The Oklahoma City Thunder (Team Spirit)*. Chicago, Ill.: Norwood House Press, 2014.

Websites
NBA History
http://www.nba.com/history
Learn more about the history of every NBA team.

Oklahoma City Thunder
http://www.nba.com/thunder
Get more information about the Thunder.

Sports Illustrated for Kids
http://www.sikids.com
Play games and read about sports.

INDEX